The

8

Minute

GUTS
BUILDER

**A Portable
Coach to
Pump
Up Your
Courage**

written by **Karen Salmansohn** illustrated by **Ellen Weinstein**

Simon & Schuster

New York   London   Toronto   Sydney

Simon & Schuster
Rockefeller Center
1230 Avenue of the Americas
New York, NY 10020

Concept and packaging by Karen Salmansohn/Glee Industries
Text copyright © 2004 by Karen Salmansohn
Illustrations and design copyright © 2004 by Ellen Weinstein

SIMON & SCHUSTER and colophon are registered trademarks
of Simon & Schuster, Inc.

For information regarding special discounts for bulk purchases,
please contact Simon & Schuster Special Sales at 1-800-456-6798
or business@simonandschuster.com

Designed by Ellen Weinstein

Manufactured in the United States of America
1   3   5   7   9   10   8   6   4   2

Library of Congress Cataloging-in-Publication data is available.

ISBN 0-7432-5557-7

The

8

Minute

GUTS
BUILDER

Intro-
duction

Pick up that phone and make that call!

Run circles around your competition!

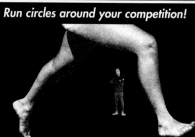

Open that closed door to your boss's office!

Turn over a new leaf!

Ever wish you had stronger guts so you could confidently:

- **Open that closed door to your boss's office**

- **Pick up that phone and make that call**

- **Carry extra weight at work**

- **Tackle a heavy problem**

- **Walk that extra distance**

- **Stop a moving train of negative thoughts**

- **Open a jam-closed heart**

Stop a moving train of negative thoughts!

Step up on that soapbox!

Stomach more than ever before!

Lift that ton of office work!

Walk down that aisle!

Open a jam-closed heart!

- Walk down that aisle

- Step up on that soapbox

- Take a sucker punch and keep on fighting

- Close a door behind you

- Turn over a new leaf

- Put down that pint of Häagen-Dazs

- Run circles around your competition

- Lift that ton of office work

- Be faster on your feet

- Stomach more than ever before

Well, if so, I've got great news.

Within a speedy 8 minutes, I'll show you how to take your guts from weak to peak, using "psyche-chology," a unique guts semantical empowering system that will miraculously give you stronger guts fast, when you need them fast:

- At your office
- In a bar
- On a date
- At a family function (or would that be family "dysfunction"?)

And these speedy 8-minutes' worth of exercise not only strengthen your guts through subtle emotional movements, they . . .

- Strengthen your spine, so your backbone will be stronger than ever

- Fortify your limbs so you'll have more strength to go out on a limb when the need strikes

- Tone up sagging spirits

- Firm up limp dreams

- Toughen up fragile hopes

  (Cool, huh?)

Friends and family will be impressed by the new, stronger, gutsier you! Soon you'll be walking taller—and against yellow lights,

because, hear, you've got the stuff to make it to the other side of that damn street—and, if not, you've got the guts to deal with being caught mid-traffic. What of it, man? So if you're ready to get the stronger guts you've been dreaming about, *wake up and stop dreaming!* Start doing these exercises!

Warm-up
Stretch

Get ready. You are now about to stretch yourself in a new and unfamiliar way.

You'll be pushing yourself past your present comfort zone—in words or deeds. To do this stretching exercise you need: pen, paper, and peace of mind. And in case you don't have paper handy, we've supplied a log where you can do *all* your writing.

pen

Speaking of . . . turn to page 86 right now, and write down the exact thing that you want but don't presently have. Be specific. Entitle what you've written: GOAL. Stare at your goal. Then return here . . .

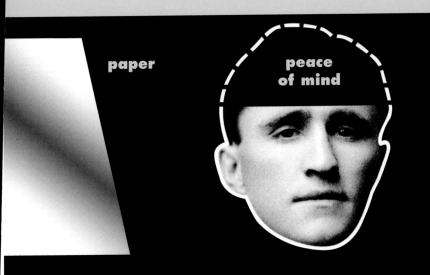

paper

peace
of mind

and stare at this:

"The reasonable man adapts himself to the world; the unreasonable man persists in trying to adapt the world to himself. Therefore, all progress depends on the unreasonable man."

—George Bernard Shaw

Sit up and take notice of
why **you want your goal.**

Do Some Sit-ups

exercise 2
(45 seconds)

1

Know this: A strong enough *why* helps
you build up your guts and commit 100%.
Go to page 87 in the log, and list 10
reasons why you'd be excited to get
your goal. A good way to increase
your heart rate with excitement is to
think about your favorite things,

%

feelings, people, events, then *link* how
your goal will get you more of all of it!
(Note: By now your heart should be
beating very fast . . . and, best of all, you
should now be remembering that, eureka,
you have a heart!)

Sit down and think about what you *won't* stand for.

Do Some Sit Downs

exercise 3
(45 seconds)

Go to page 88 in the log, and make a list of 10 things that you despise or that piss you off— and link *not* getting what you want to this list. Make yourself angry. Disturbed.

Annoyed. Work up a sweat. Get your blood flowing. Remember: Pain and anger and irritation can be your pals — *but only if* you use them as motivators.

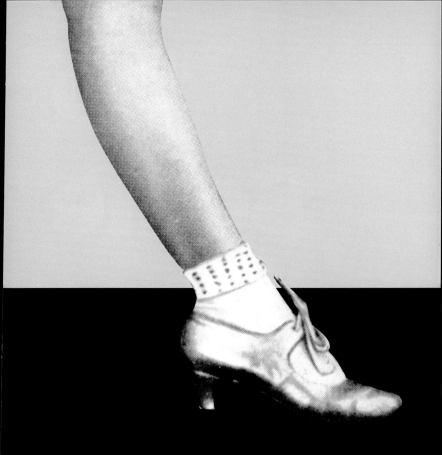

And here's the catch: You can't stay focused on what bums you out. You must move your bum past pain, anger, irritation toward getting your goal.

Do Some But Kicks

Are you sitting on a big *But*?

Kick These *Buts* Now!

"But I shouldn't bug
my boss for that raise."
"But I'm too old."
"But I'm too young."
"But I'm too nervous
to talk to that hottie
at the bar."
"But, but, but,
but . . . "

YES!

It's time to kick that big *But* out of your way

YES!

by reminding yourself that much of what you

YES!

tell yourself are "mythtakes"—myths that

YES!

foolishly hold you back.

Remember: Before Roger Bannister came along, nobody thought it was possible to run a

-minute mile,

so nobody did. Then Roger Bannister ran a 4-minute mile—and now so many folks run 4-minute miles it's run-of-the-mill.

Do Chest-Weight Lifts

exercise 5
(30 seconds)

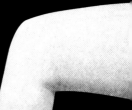

Lift the weight of your fears off your chest.

Go to page 89 in the log, and list what you fear are the worst (and non-mythtake) things that can happen if you go for what you want . . . and be sure to separate your list into 2 categories:

LIST 1: FEARS THAT ARE THINGS YOU CAN CONTROL.

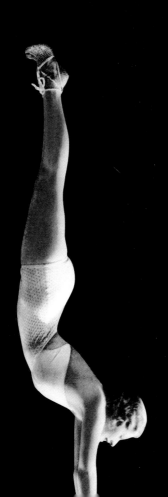

Now, come up with a game plan for list 1:
Address your fears—then send your fears
packing to a new address . . . far away
from *you* by coming up with solutions and
staying determined to get your goal.

Your chest-weight-lift mantra:

Defocus on fears

Refocus on goal.

As Henry Ford once said: *"Obstacles are those frightful things you see when you take your eyes off your goal."*

Expec-tation Lifts

exercise 6
(15 seconds)

Build up your winner muscles, not your whiner muscles.

Expectation lifts come . . .

WHAT I WANT

Step1: First, you must lift something you might not have lifted in years—your standards. Step 2: Once your standards are raised high, be sure to keep them there. Now, raise your expectations for your life up, up, up to reach the same towering level as your standards.

in two successive steps.

WHAT I'LL GET

Decide now: You *are* a winner. You *are* an achiever. You *are* 110% committed to creating a life of joy, evolution, and elevated standards. As Bertolt Brecht once said: "Do not fear death so much but rather the inadequate life."

Do Some Boot- strap Pull-ups

Increase your guts power
by increasing your usage of
powerful, gutsy words.

Mark Twain believed that the right words worked as powerful agents: "Whenever we come upon one of those intensely right words . . ." said Mark, "the resulting effect is physical as well as spiritual, and electrically prompt." Well, mark Mark's words—he was right!

You increase your personal power by increasing the power of the words you associate with your identity.

Choose your favorite
powerful words
from this menu,
then link these
words to a noun
that represents
your goal.
(For instance, if you
want to be a musician,
tell yourself "I'm the
goddess of alternative
rock.")

Kick-butt

Extraordinary

Killer

WORLD-CLASS

Goddess of

Cindy Crawford of

𝕲𝖔𝖉 𝖔𝖋

Sorcerer of

Master of

Mistress of

Obstacle Jumps

You know the ropes . . . and how to jump high and jump fast!

exercise 8
(30 seconds)

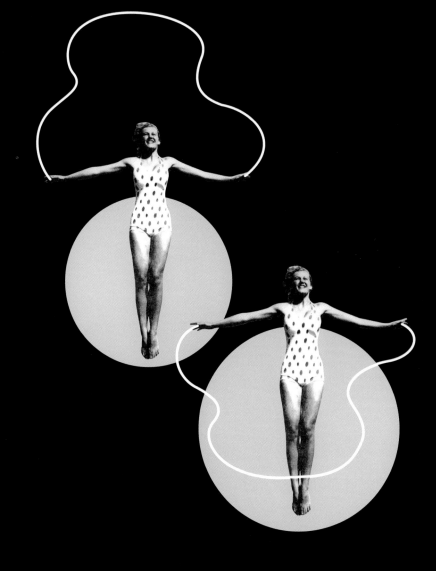

You've jumped many obstacles before . . .
remember? Go to page 90 in the log and
for the next 30 seconds list memories of
courage to give you lasting courage.
Remember: All those obstacles appeared
big at first . . . and now look so small.

COCKYTALE

For quick energy jolts, prepare and store away an energizing "cockytale" —a quickie tale of an amazing obstacle jump that you can indulge in when you need to make yourself feel super cocky quickly! Remember: High self-esteem is the opposite of fear.

Do One Shoulder Stand

Climb up on the pedestal and onto the shoulders of someone who has what you want.

See life
from her
point of
view.
Remind
yourself why
you're just
as good
as she is
and deserve
everything
she has,
dammit.
Now close
your eyes
and imagine
you are her.

Breathe like her. Stand like her. Hold yourself tall like her. Psychologists believe that borrowing somebody's physiology can actually be very empowering for garnering more courage.

Use a Punch-ing Bag

exercise 10
(30 seconds)

They say, "Success is the best revenge." Well, they is right.

Channel your competitive spirit into moving you forward. Think about someone you wanna piss off by getting your goal. Or think about somebody who you feel dislikes you or doesn't believe in you—and how gleeful you'll feel when he discovers you've gotten your goal.

Keep in mind what Aristotle once said:

"It concerns us to know the purposes we seek in life, for then, like archers aiming at a definite mark, we shall be more likely to attain what we want."

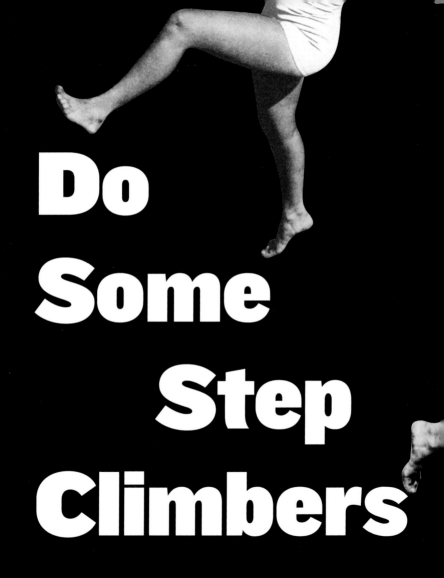

Do
Some
Step
Climbers

exercise 11
(90 seconds)
**Take small steps
forward . . .
and don't pull
your guts out
moving too fast.**

First, go to page 91
in the log, and take
60 seconds to write a
clear, step-by-step plan
of all the things you
must do—and *actually can
do* . . . meaning, things that
are truly in your control.
Then take 30 seconds to think
about how you can do these
things in 3-step chunks. If
a particular step is *very*
large, take 20 seconds
to break this step
down into a smaller
3-step chunk.

Finally, take 10 seconds to think about this.

"True life is lived when tiny changes occur."
—Leo Tolstoy

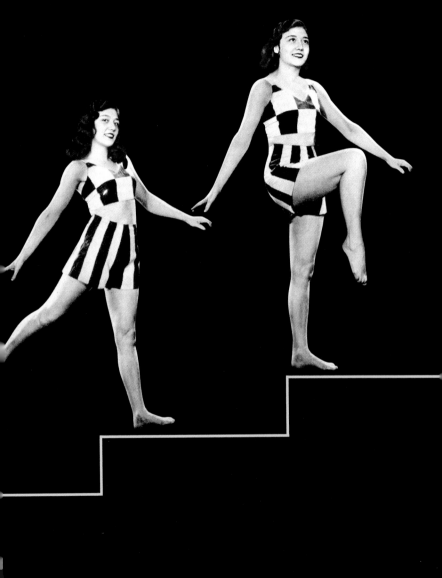

Run!
Run!
Run!

exercise 12
(30 seconds)

**Run, run, run your plan
through your mind.**

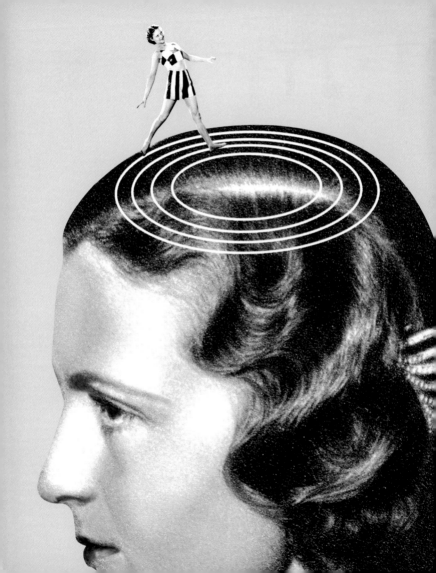

Focus on what you want
so strongly that you can
visualize every detail of
having it so clearly, your
goal becomes a little
movie in your mind: a
Goal Mental Rental.
Replay your Goal
Mental Rental over and
over until you know the
goal climax scenes
by heart—and feel you've
achieved them deeply in
your heart. Run, run, run
this through your mind
as well: Conceive it and
believe it—and you *will*
receive it.

Do Some Life Cycling

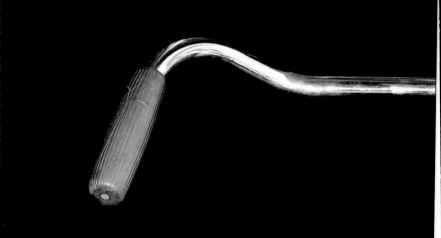

Your life odometer is turning over a bit more each day. Be sure you're enjoying the ride.

exercise 13
(20 seconds)

1825 days
12 hours

Life meter

In 365 days you'll be a year older. In 2,190 days: 6 years older. In 21,535 days: 59 years older . . . and maybe even dead! So . . . how do you want to be remembered? Visualize your true *end goal results:* how you want to be thought about at the end of your lifetime! Keep in mind what John Ruskin said: "The highest reward for a person's toil is not what they get for it, but what they become by it." Now with *all* this in mind, decide to rename *failure* as *fullure*—full of things you learn—and guts-building empowerers that make you *stronger* to achieve lots of **goals** in your lifetime! And if you *do* get what you want, you must learn from *this,* too! You must see "winning experiences" as "in-periences"—lessons you take into your system and guts—and further build up your **personal power!**

Do a Little Hula of Joy

exercise 14
(5 seconds)

Jump up and down and celebrate ahead of time for what you're about to do. You are a winner because you're not letting your fears guide you . . . you're being guided by your passions. As Anaïs Nin once said: "Life shrinks or expands according to your courage." By building up your guts, you're expanding your life. *Congratulations! Now go get 'em, killer!*

Training Log

Log

Keep track of your gut-building progress in the following log . . .

Warm-up Stretch

Sit Downs

Chest-Weight Lifts

Obstacle Jumps

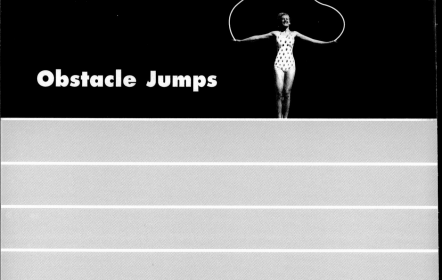

Step Climbers

The Authorized Bibliography of Karen Salmansohn

50% Off: A Novel of Love in the Age of Packaging

How to Make Your Man Behave in 21 Days or Less, Using the Secrets of Professional Dog Trainers

How to Succeed in Business Without a Penis: Secrets and Strategies for the Working Woman

The 30-Day Plan to Whip Your Career into Submission: Transform Yourself from Job Slave into Master of Your Destiny in Just One Month

Even God Is Single (So Stop Giving Me a Hard Time): The Book Every Single Single Girl Needs to Defend Against Nudgy Family and Friends

I Don't Need to Have Children, I Date Them: 23 Child Psychology Techniques to Use on Boys of All Ages

The Burn Your Anger Book: Write It, Rip It, Torch It

How to Be Happy, Dammit: A Cynic's Guide to Spiritual Happiness

The Clitourist: A Guide to One of the Hottest Spots on Earth

How to Speak Fluent Lovey-Dovey in 11 Languages in 24 Hours

Hot Mama: How to Have a Babe and Be a Babe

The Petit Connoisseur series: Art, Fashion, Golf

The 7 Lively Sins: How to Enjoy Your Life, Dammit

Quickie Stickies: 100 New Edgy Inspirations for When You're Feeling Unglued

How to Change Your Entire Life by Doing Absolutely Nothing: 10 Do-Nothing Relaxation Exercises to Calm You Down Quickly So You Can Speed Forward Faster

(Phew. Is she exhausted.)

KAREN SALMANSOHN is the author of many bestselling and "new edgy" books (look left) and products (lookie right here), such as *Good Karma in a Box; Unavailable: It's More Than a Perfume, It's a Philosophy;* and the *Mr. Right When You Need Him* doll kit. Plus she is the writer/illustrator of the 'tween series Alexandra Rambles On. She's also the founder of Amazon Girl, Inc. and Glee Industries, both agencies specializing in packaging books and products. She gives motivational talks nationally and internationally (and locally to friends on the phone!).

ELLEN WEINSTEIN is an illustrator whose work has appeared on book covers, theater posters, and in many publications, including *Time, The New York Times,* and *The Wall Street Journal.* She illustrated and designed the book *Quickie Stickies: 100 New Edgy Inspirations for When You're Feeling Unglued,* also written by Karen Salmansohn. You can see more of her work at www.ellenweinstein.com.